MOTORCYCLES!

By Barry Armitage

To Abbie, with love

Photo Credits
A special thanks to the manufacturers and organizations who provided photos for this book:
BMW of North America, Inc., Kerker Exhausts, Benelli/Moto Guzzi North America, KTM America,
Parabellum (Rifle Fairings), Harley-Davidson, Inc., and Daytona International Speedway.

Cover photo: Daytona International Speedway

Additional photos by: Terry Ellifritz, Bill Wood, and Greg Harrison.

Library of Congress Cataloging-in-Publication Data

Armitage, Barry.
    Motorcycles / by Barry Armitage.
       p. cm.
    Includes index.
    Summary: Introduces different types of motorcycles, riding
techniques, and the world of motorcycle racing, from motocross,
speedway, and drag racing to desert and ice racing.
    ISBN 0-8069-6892-3 (pbk.)
    1. Motorcycles—Juvenile literature. 2. Motorcycle racing–
–Juvenile literature. [1. Motorcycles. 2. Motorcycle racing.]
I. Title.   88-16964
TL440.A745   1988   CIP
629.2′275—dc19   AC

3 5 7 9 10 8 6 4 2

Published in 1988 by Sterling Publishing Co., Inc.
Two Park Avenue, New York, N.Y. 10016
First published in paperback in 1988 by Willowisp Press, Inc., Ohio
Copyright © 1988 by Willowisp Press, Inc.
Distributed in Canada by Oak Tree Press Ltd.
℅ Canadian Manda Group, P.O. Box 920, Station U
Toronto, Ontario, Canada M8Z 5P9
Distributed in Great Britain and Europe by Cassell PLC
Artillery House, Artillery Row, London SW1P 1RT, England
Distributed in Australia by Capricorn Ltd.
P.O. Box 665, Lane Cove, NSW 2066
Manufactured in the United States of America
All rights reserved

Sterling ISBN 0-8069-6892-3 Trade

CONTENTS

MOTORCYCLES—
EXCITEMENT IN MOTION

These street bikes are as fast as the racing bikes of a few years ago. Now bikers can feel the thrill of speed and safety at the same time!

You hear a faraway rumbling. It grows louder, and you know that something different is coming closer. You turn and see—a motorcycle!

If you like to feel the sensation of motion with your whole body, then you'll love motorcycling! You'll feel the wind in your face as you whip along the street. Off the road, riding cross-country, you can pull up on the handlebars and feel the thrill of jumping 10 or 15 feet (3 or 4½ meters) over a log or stream.

5

MOTORCYCLES WORK HARD AND PLAY HARD

People like motorcycles for many reasons. Bikes are easy to park and can cut through and around stalled traffic easily. They cost less to buy and maintain than most cars do. And you can learn to do a lot of your own bike maintenance. That's important when you're exploring isolated country locations, far from the nearest repair shop.

But most of all, bikes are fun to ride! When you ride one properly and with the right equipment, motorcycle riding is safe. Be sure to read the important safety tips that appear later in this book before you start biking!

Bikes come in a wide variety of styles, and you can choose one to meet your own needs. Most bikes you see on the road are street bikes. There are several types of street bikes. Big touring bikes (tourers), like the one in the above photo, can cruise for hours. They can carry two people (three with a sidecar) and lots of equipment. You'll notice that tourers have a tall windshield called a fairing. The fairing protects both the rider and the passenger from rain and wind. The tourer's big engine gives it lots of power to speed along and to carry heavy loads. Often, police motorcycles are specially equipped tourers.

Brightly colored, small bikes with small windshields are called street racers. Riders choose them because they're fast, light, and fun to ride— like sports cars.

Another kind of street bike is the cruiser. The cruiser has a low seat, and the handlebars are higher than most other types of bikes. Cruisers usually don't have windshields, so they aren't very comfortable for long rides on the highway. But they're great for cruising around town.

BUILT FOR POWER!

Motorcycles are carefully designed to be as fast, powerful, and safe as possible. Then they are tested over and over again to make sure that the design works.

Motorcycles have engines that are smaller and lighter than the engines in cars. Because motorcycles weigh less than cars, they don't need big engines.

The best way to compare motorcycle engines is by size. The size of an engine is measured in cubic centimeters (cc). The larger the engine, the more powerful it is. An engine that is 250 cc is larger and more powerful than an engine that is 100 cc.

The motorcycle's frame has to be strong enough to hold the bike together, but light enough not to slow the bike down. Frames used to be made of steel tubes welded together, like a bicycle frame. Today, many frames for motorcycles are molded from aluminum, which provides the needed strength and lightness.

Brakes on a motorcycle are much like those on cars, only smaller. Older bikes use drum brakes. These are pads that rub against the inside of metal drums on each wheel. Newer bikes and cars use disc brakes. They have a special pad that grips a disc attached to each wheel. Disc brakes work well even when they're hot. And in motorcycle races, the brakes can really get hot!

The steering mechanism on a motorcycle turns the bike the way the driver wants it to go. But just turning the handlebars doesn't do the whole job. When turning a corner, a motorcycle rider must lean into the turn to be sure the machine turns the way he or she wants it to.

These racers are testing out the corners at the Isle of Man course. Turning a corner like this is tricky. It takes just the right combination of balance and skill.

OFF TO THE RACES!

In motorcycle racing, you'll find some of the most thrilling action you'll ever see! If there are no races near you, watch for a listing of bike races on television.

Sometimes riders race on street bikes that have been made lighter and more powerful for racing. But most riders buy a racing bike that is designed just for racing. Racing bikes are faster and lighter in weight than street bikes. And the engine is louder and more powerful.

MOTOCROSS— CHILLS, THRILLS, AND SPILLS

If you see motorcycles flying through the air during a race, it must be a motocross race. Motocross is the most popular form of bike competition in the world. The race takes place on a winding dirt track. Big jumps and tight turns make it hard for the riders to stay on their bikes.

Bikes like these (left and below) are popular for motocross and enduro events. Daring jumps and tight turns are all part of the thrills of off-road racing!

A motocross race is run for a set length of time. When the time is up, each of the first ten riders wins points. First place gets one point, second gets two, and so on. Two races are run, and the rider with the lowest score wins. Kids as young as four years old can race special, small bikes in motocross events.

The start of a motocross race is especially exciting. A metal bar, which holds all the racers at the starting line, flips down, and the riders roar off together. Sometimes there's an accident when all the bikes try to squeeze together around the first corner. But usually no one is hurt. Often, when riders fall, they get on their bikes again and blast back into the pack.

SUPERCROSS—

BIG JUMPS, BIG MONEY FOR WINNERS

Supercross is a professional motocross event held in a big sports arena. Since the course must be short, there are *huge* jumps of 15 feet (4½ meters) or more, and a lot of tight turns. Only very experienced, professional riders should attempt big jumps. Younger riders should stick to regular motocross.

13

It's a bird, it's a plane, it's a motorcycle! Rocket-fast motorcycles like these (above and left) go over 300 miles per hour!!

FASTER
AND FASTER

There have been speed records as long as there have been motorcycles. The record today stands at 318 mph (509 km/h). Bikes built to break speed records look more like airplanes. Some are so long and skinny that the bikers must lie down to fit inside.

The Bonneville Salt Flats in Utah are used for most speed attempts. These dry salt beds offer a safe place to set new records because they are wide and flat and there's a lot of room for the motorcycles to slow down and stop.

The riders of Formula One bikes (above) are some of the best in the world.
Formula Two bikes (below) are almost as fast as Formula Ones and take
just as much skill to race.

Racing fans love the Superbikes! Superbikes are a lot like the motorcycles that fans themselves ride on the street.

THE SUPER RACES— DAYTONA AND THE ISLE OF MAN

Each spring, riders come from as far away as Australia to race at Daytona International Speedway's *Speed Week* in Florida. This is one of the most famous series of motorcycle races in the world.

The main Daytona event is a 200-mile (320-kilometer) race for bikes up to 750 cc. These motorcycles are almost like the bikes you see on highways every day. They're called Superbikes, because they're regular motorcycles that have been modified to make them very fast. Race fans love the Superbike races, since they can cheer for motorcycles that are like the ones they own.

Formula One bikes also race at Daytona. They are the fastest road-racing motorcycles. Designed just for racing, they can go over 200 mph (320 km/h)! Like Indianapolis race cars, these bikes are too fast and loud to be allowed on the streets. Since they're made for racing, they're light—just 350 pounds (157½ kilograms). Street bikes weigh over 600 pounds (270 kilograms). Lighter bikes move fast, stop fast, and use less gas.

Superbike rider Freddie Spencer shows off his knee-dragging, cornering style aboard his Honda.

Formula Two bikes race at Daytona, too. These racing bikes have engines up to 250 cc. They can go faster than 150 mph (240 km/h).

The oldest and most famous road race in the world takes place off the coast of England on the Isle of Man. In the Isle of Man Tourist Trophy (TT) race, all types of street bikes and racing bikes run a set number of laps on a 37-mile (59-kilometer) course marked out on regular roads.

Bikers who enter races at Daytona and the Isle of Man are the best riders in the world. And good riders make sure they are safe riders. They wear the proper protective clothing: leather suits, gloves, and boots. They *always* wear helmets. Road racers wear knee pads, too. The knee pads protect their knees if they scrape the pavement when they go around corners. If there is an accident, the clothing, boots, or helmet may be ruined. But the rider is safe.

When you bike, do it like a pro. NEVER go without your protective clothing.

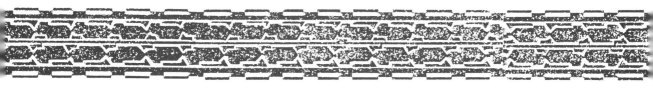

Leather suits, helmets, gloves, and boots are all standard equipment for these Superbike champions. All motorcycle riders should make sure they wear the proper protective clothing.

DESERT RACING—
ONLY THE TOUGHEST
NEED APPLY

Desert racing is one of the most challenging motorcycle sports around today. This event, which follows a long, tough course laid out in the desert, may last hours, days, or even weeks.

The superbig desert bikes can travel over 100 mph (160 km/h). But some of the course is off-road, so the bikes have to be able to jump over rocks and logs like motocross bikes.

On long desert races, the riders are allowed to rest at night. In the morning, they leave in the same order in which they arrived. This way, a rider who is ahead doesn't lose his or her place by stopping to sleep.

The most famous off-road race for motorcycles is the Paris to Dakar Rally. The rally is 8,000 miles (12,800 kilometers) long. It starts in Paris, France, and runs to Dakar, Senegal, in Africa. The race lasts several weeks, but many of the bikes break down and never make it to the finish line.

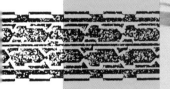

DIRT TRACKIN'

If you like action, you'll love dirt-track motorcycle races. These races began in America, but they're now popular in Europe and Japan. Hundreds of oval dirt tracks in the United States are used for horse racing. Motorcycle riders soon discovered that the horse racetracks were great places to race bikes, and the sport of dirt-track racing was born. Most of the great racers in America started as dirt trackers.

Dirt-track races are run on tracks that are a mile (1.6 kilometers), a half mile (.8 kilometer), or a quarter mile (.4 kilometer) or less in length. Riders practice on the day of the race. Then they are timed one by one. The riders with the fastest times are chosen to fill up several rounds of competition, called heats. These heats are usually ten laps. The top three finishers in each heat compete in the final.

In the final race, the riders line up and rev their engines. When the starting light turns green, they take off toward the first turn. The bike that makes the turn first has the best chance to win. The racers have to put one foot down on the ground while turning to keep their bikes from falling over. Speed during the straight sections on the mile tracks reaches over 130 mph (208 km/h) with these 750-cc bikes.

The steeplechase is another type of race held on a dirt track. (In the United States, a steeplechase is also called a tourist trophy or TT.) In a steeplechase, something special is added to the oval track. Instead of racing on a perfect oval, the riders turn off the track and enter the infield (center section). There, the riders go over a jump. The big dirt trackers fly ten feet into the air!

Dirt bikes for racetracks are built only to race. They cost less than other racing bikes, because they use engines that are fairly standard. These motorcycles don't have starters, lights, or other equipment that a street bike has, and this keeps them light and fast. They have tires with bumps all over them that grip the dirt during turns.

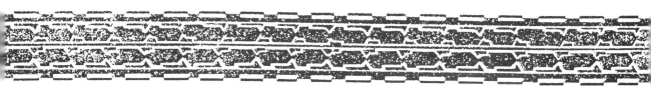

NOTHING'S LOUDER THAN DRAG RACING

Drag racing is the loudest kind of motorcycle race! In drag racing, racers vroom off two by two on a quarter-mile (.4-kilometer) straight track. The motorcycle with the fastest time from start to finish wins the race. The best bikes go more than 200 mph (320 km/h).

Drag-racing bikes are specially designed for short bursts of speed. Riders change gears quickly by pushing a button.

Drag racing engines are super-powered. Some drag-racing bikes use two engines, and some even use car engines.

Because the bikes are so long and low to the ground, and their engines are so powerful, a special drag bar is attached to the end of the bike. The drag bar balances the bike so that it does not turn over or pop a wheelie as the bike's powerful engine pushes it ahead.

TRIALS—
A TEST OF
BALANCE
AND CONTROL

In trials competition, contestants compete against tough obstacles. The winner is the rider who can follow a path over large rocks, logs, and steep trails without losing his balance and having to put his foot down on the ground. Trials bikes look like small motocross cycles. Since they don't have to go fast or go far, they have small engines and gas tanks. Many have tiny seats, since the rider usually stands up on the footpegs to help balance the bike. Some riders practice for trials by riding over old cars!

Rocks, streams, hills, cliffs, and boulders—the Trials racer has to face it all!

ENDUROS ARE ROUGH RIDING

Enduros are off-road competitions run on a path marked by arrows stapled to trees. The course is rough. It is run for several miles through the worst mud holes and up the steepest hills in the area. The object of an enduro is not to be the fastest racer. Instead, the enduro rider must arrive at certain checkpoints at specified times. Points are given to a rider for being early or late at each checkpoint. The rider with the lowest score wins.

Enduro bikes look a lot like motocross bikes. They have tires with bumps on them to give them a good grip. Their high fenders keep mud and sticks from jamming the wheels. Enduro competitions are held for many levels of riders, so it's easy to find an enduro with others who have your level of experience.

SPEEDWAY AND ICE RACING – FAST AND FURIOUS

In speedway racing, small, fast bikes race on oval dirt tracks inside an arena.

Speedway racing is loud and exciting, and it's one of the most popular forms of motorcycle racing in the world.

Since the races are short, these small and light bikes have tiny gas tanks. They use alcohol instead of gasoline, which makes them superfast.

In speedway, a series of five races is run. Three points are awarded for first place, two points for second, and one point for third. The rider with the most points at the end of five races wins.

Ice racing isn't as slippery as it looks. Tires with spikes help keep the bikes from sliding.

Only real daredevils try ice racing. Ice-racing bikes look a lot like speedway motorcycles, but they have metal studs or spikes in the tires to help the bike grip the ice. The races usually are short, so riders don't get too cold. Sidecar motorcycles also race on ice.

GLOSSARY

cc short for cubic centimeter, a measurement of volume used to compare engine sizes.

cruiser motorcycle with a custom design. Cruisers usually have handlebars, a small gas tank, and a low-slung seat.

desert racing competitive events covering a marked course over dry, rough areas, lasting several hours to several weeks. Enduro-type bikes are used.

dirt track races held on oval or modified oval tracks on two-cylinder bikes ranging up to 750 cc. Different bikes are approved for separate classes.

drag racing competition where two motorcycles race against each other over a straight quarter-mile (.4-kilometer) track.

enduro a timed competition run over a marked course running many miles through rough off-road areas. Riders try to arrive at checkpoints at a specified time. If a rider arrives either too early or too late, he gains points. The low score wins.

fairing a big windshield on touring motorcycles to protect riders from wind and rain; usually made of fiberglass or plastic.

Formula One specially built race bikes with engines up to 500 cc that compete in grand prix and similar events. Formula One bikes are the most advanced road-race bikes.

Formula Two   similar to Formula One, but limited to 250-cc engine sizes.

ice racers   similar to speedway bikes, but with studded or spiked tires to grip ice.

motocross   a race run for a fixed period of time over a repeating course with many turns and jumps.

sidecar   a pod with an extra wheel and space for an extra passenger attached to the side of a motorcycle.

speedway motorcycles   small, brakeless, race bikes that run on alcohol for indoor events on dirt oval tracks.

street racers   regular motorcycles designed to look and perform more like race bikes. Sometimes called café racers.

Superbikes   racing motorcycles based on regular street designs up to 750 cc.

supercross   a professional motocross race run in a stadium. Supercross uses a shorter course with more jumps and turns than a motocross event.

tourer   motorcycles designed for long-distance traveling, usually with a fairing.

trials   motorcycle competition in which riders attempt to ride over various obstacles without losing their balance and placing a foot down.

TT   short for Tourist Trophy. Used to describe two types of races: the annual Isle of Man road races and the dirt-track races using jumps that are also called steeplechase.

INDEX